FIND
THE
CAT AND MORE!
Volume 2

By Cindy Olejar
2014

One of the intentions when reading this book is to practice using prepositions to say where the cat is located compared to the other objects in the photos.

You can also find other objects in the pictures once the cat is found! Be creative!

Some prepositions:
above, across, against, along, among, around, at, behind, below, beneath, beside, between, beyond, by, in, near, next to, on, over, through, to, toward, under, upon, within

Where is the cat?

The cat is **under** the table.

The cat is **behind** the dog.

Where is the cat?

The cat is **in** the planter.

The cat is **above** the porch.

The cat is **near** the window.

Where is the cat?

The cat is **in front of** the window.

The cat is **on** the table.

The cat is **next to** the chair.

Where is the cat?

The cat is **in** the cat bed.

The cat is **next to** the toy mouse.

Where is the cat?

The cat is **behind** the curtain.

The cat is **on** the carpet.

Where is the cat?

The cat is **in front of** the bush.

The cat is **by** the sidewalk.

The cat is **near** the grass.

Where is the cat?

The cat is **on** the tree stump.

The cat is **above** the ground.

Where is the cat?

The cat is **under** the chair.

The cat is **on** the floor.

Where is the cat?

The cat is **on** the steps.

The cat is **in between** the banisters.

Where is the cat?

The cat is **in front of** the door.

The cat is **above** the steps.

Where is the cat?

The cat is **on** the bed.

The cat is **next to** the lamp.

The cat is **between** the pillow and the lamp.

Where is the cat?

The black cat is **up on** the ledge.

The white and black cat is **on** the porch.

Where is the cat?

The cat is **in** the window.

The cat is **near** the plant.

Where is the cat?

The cat is **on** the pillow.

The cat is **near** the window.

The cat is **above** the dog crate.

Where is the cat?

The cat is **on** the bed.

The cat is **next to** the pillow.

Where is the cat?

The cat is **behind** the curtain.

The cat is **near** the fan.

The cat is **against** the window.

Where is the cat?

The cat is **between** the tree and picnic table.

The cat is standing **on** the ground.

The cat is **in** the yard.

Where is the cat?

The cat is **on** the bed.

The cat is **against** the covers.

The cat is **near** the pillows.

Where is the cat?

The cat is **on** the table.

The cat is **near** the couch.

The cat is **above** the ground.

Where is the cat?

The cat is **in** his perch.

The cat is **in front of** the window.

Where is the cat?

The cat is **on** the blanket.

The cat is **near** the dog.

The cat is **next to** the wall.

Where is the cat?

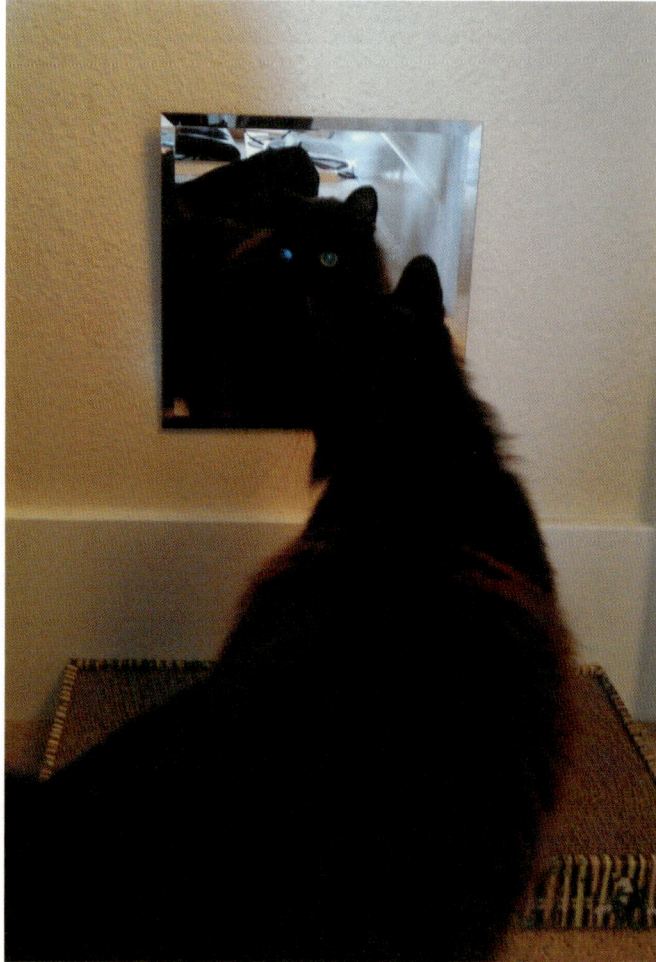

The cat is **in front** of the mirror.

The cat is **in** the mirror!

Where is the cat?

The cat is **next to** the banister.

The cat is **next to** the bush.

The cat is **near** the tree.

Where is the cat?

The cat is **between** the trees.

The cat is **at** the bottom of the steps.

Where is the cat?

The cat is **above** the stairs.

The cat is **on** his cat perch.

Where is the cat?

The cat is **near** the blue door.

The cat is **behind** the bicycle tire.

The cat is **on** the porch.

Where is the cat?

The cat is **on top of** the fence.

The cat is **on** the fence.

The cat is **upon** the fence.

Where is the cat?

The cat is **on** the steps.

The cat is **near** the porch.

Where is the cat?

The cat is **on** the bed.

The cat is **next to** the dog.

The cat is **by** the wall.

Where is the cat?

The cat is **in front of** the ivy bush.

The cat is **on** the sidewalk.

Where is the cat?

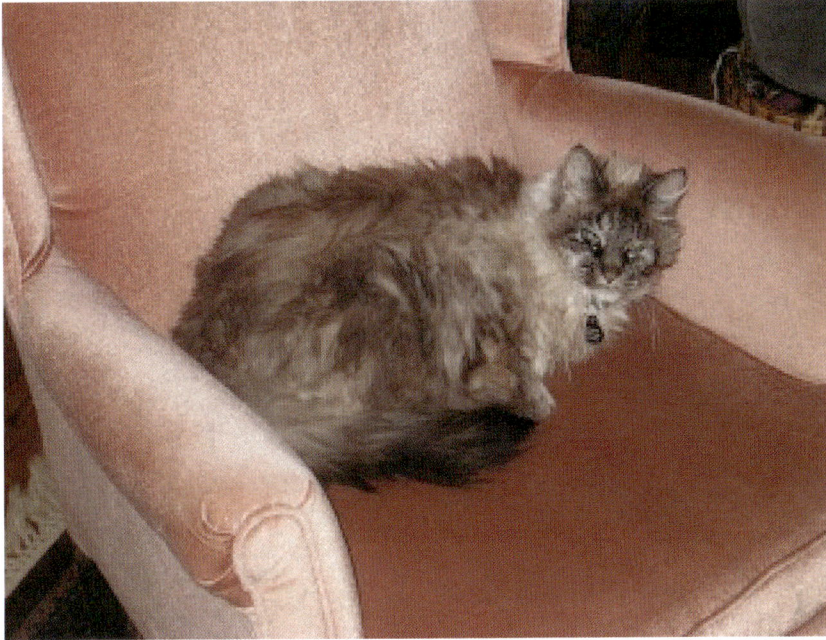

The cat is _____ the chair.

Where is the cat?

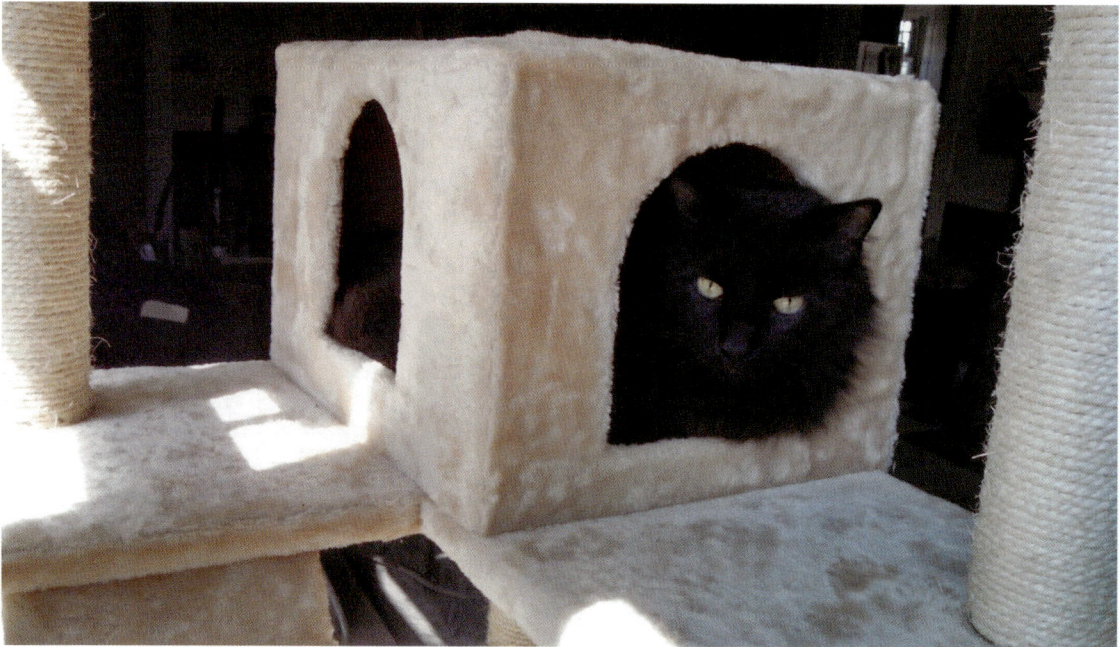

The cat is ____ the cat house.

Where is the cat?

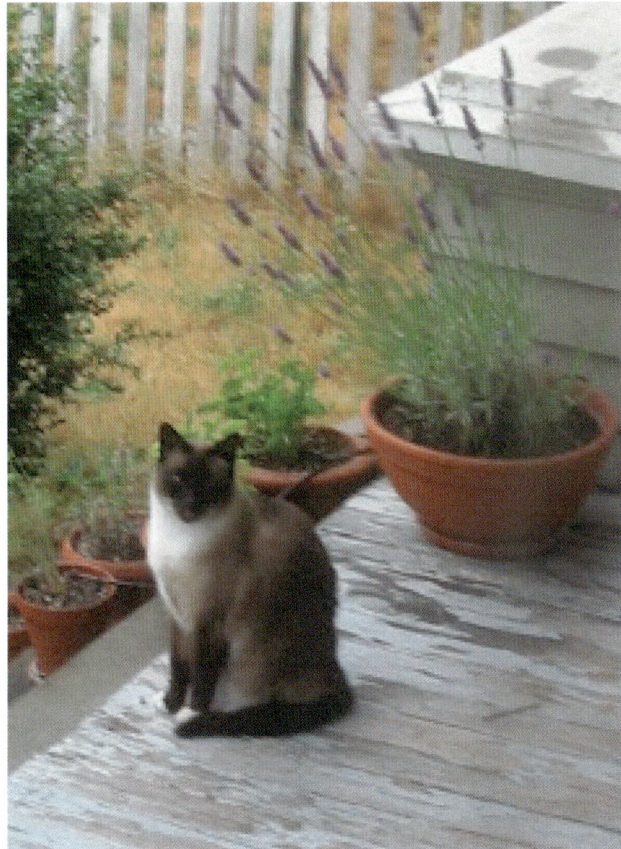

The cat is ____ the porch.

The cat is _____ the plant.

Where is the cat?

The cat is riding _____ the stroller.

Where is the cat?

The cat is _____ the ottoman.

The cat is _____ the window.

I hope you had fun finding the cat!

If you go walking look to see if you can find any cats!

Meow!

Cindy Olejar lives in Seattle, WA. To contact the author email cindyolejar@yahoo.com

Paste your own cat photo below or draw a picture of a cat and write a sentence saying where the cat is!

_____

_____

THE END !

Made in the USA
Charleston, SC
01 May 2015